SEP   2004

DUE

The Erie Canal

CORNERSTONES OF FREEDOM

SECOND SERIES

R. Conrad Stein

Children's Press®
A Division of Scholastic Inc.
New York • Toronto • London • Auckland • Sydney
Mexico City • New Delhi • Hong Kong
Danbury, Connecticut

Photographs © 2004: Art Resource, NY/Giraudon: 4 (Museum of the City
of New York, New York, NY); Bridgeman Art Library International Ltd.,
London/New York: 11, 45 bottom (New-York Historical Society, New York,
NY), 12 (Royal Ontario Museum, Toronto, Canada); Brown Brothers: cover
top, 26, 35, 36, 44 bottom; Corbis Images: 31, 34 (Bettmann), 32
(Museum of the City of New York), 24, 40 (Lee Snider), 23; Culver
Pictures: 5 bottom, 33, 38, 39; Courtesy of Erie Canal Museum, Syracuse,
New York: cover bottom, 3, 16, 18, 20, 22, 29, 45 center; Hulton
Archive/Getty Images: 30; Courtesy of the New York State Museum,
Albany, NY: 15; North Wind Picture Archives: 5 top, 6, 7, 9, 13, 17 right,
17 left, 21, 27, 37, 44 top, 45 top; Collection of the Rochester Public
Library, Local History Division: 28; Stock Montage, Inc.: 8; The Image
Works/Stephen D. Cannerelli/Syracuse Newspapers: 41; Courtesy of the
University of Rochester Library, Department of Rare Books & Special
Collections: 25.

Illustration p. 17 by Robert Cronan, Lucidity Information Design, LLC

Library of Congress Cataloging-in-Publication Data
Stein, R. Conrad.
  The Erie Canal / R. Conrad Stein.
      p. cm. — (Cornerstones of freedom, second series)
  Includes bibliographical references and index.
    ISBN 0-516-24243-1
    1. Erie Canal (N.Y.)—History—Juvenile literature. [1. Erie
Canal (N.Y.)—History.] I. Title. II. Cornerstones of freedom.
Second series.
F127.E5S74 2004
386'.48'09747—dc22

                                              2003023898

TO SEE A FULL THOUSAND BRAVE FELLOWS

At work among mountains so tall
To dig through the valleys so level,
Through rocks for to cut a canal.

—Lines from a song that celebrated the
thousands of workers who helped dig the
Erie Canal.

This lithograph shows an American farm in the early 1800s. At that time, many people depended on family farms, both large and small, for their livelihood.

AMERICA AND THE WEST

In the early 1800s, the United States was a young nation made up of farmers. The vast majority of those farmers lived on the sliver of land hugging the Atlantic Ocean. Only a few rugged pioneers had ventured to the West and established farms in territories such as Ohio and Illinois. Those pioneers found rich lands in the western wilderness. Why didn't more people in the East simply move west to the fertile land? Because the Appalachian Mountains stood in their way, like a jagged wall. Lovely and lonely, the mountain chain stretched from Canada to Alabama and blocked the nation's westward expansion.

The Appalachian Mountains were a barrier to early westward expansion.

The biggest passage through the Appalachians was the Cumberland Gap, near the point where Virginia, Kentucky, and Tennessee meet. But **trekking** over the Cumberland Gap and other mountain roads was hard, especially for farm families. The families needed to bring cows, chickens,

THE CUMBERLAND ROAD

In 1811, work began on the Cumberland Road, also called the National Pike or the National Road. It allowed settlers and goods to flow from the eastern states to the wilderness lands in the West. The road cut through the Appalachian Mountains at the Cumberland Gap and then snaked more than 500 miles (805 kilometers) through the wilderness. It ended at Vandalia, Illinois. The National Road was America's first "superhighway."

A wagon train makes its way along the National Road in the early 1800s. At its peak, the road was often crowded with wagon trains, horses, sheep, and even herds of cattle.

plows, and tools in order to establish new farms in the West. Taking farm tools and livestock through the rugged mountains was a very difficult task.

Once a farm family managed to cross into the western lands, it faced another problem: where to sell its farm produce. Wheat brought a fair price in settled states, such as New York and Massachusetts. There, working people were willing to pay for farm products. But shipping bags of wheat or flour back east by horse-drawn wagons meant recrossing the Appalachians. This was an expensive process that cut into the farmer's profits.

The cheapest way to transport people and goods was by water. Riverboats operated on many of the nation's rivers and inland waterways. The boats could be likened to

Passengers, horses, and cattle ride a small boat down the Ohio River.

Noah's Ark. They carried mooing cows, barking dogs, crates of chickens, and pioneer families. Rivers in the Appalachians were mainly swift-moving streams that carried canoes and other small craft.

A few Americans suggested building a canal—an artificial river—through the mountain chain. Impossible, said expert engineers. Digging a waterway to pierce the Appalachians was a dream, and a foolish one at that. The idea of such a canal was proposed to President Thomas Jefferson. He said, "It [the canal] is a splendid project and may be executed a century hence, but it is a little short of madness to think of it at this day."

President Thomas Jefferson referred to the idea of building a canal as "a little short of madness."

THE DREAMERS

The summer of 1777 was a **dismal** one for what would become the United States. At the time, the nation was fighting England in a bloody war for independence. The Americans were losing badly. Ragtag American armies retreated on all fronts while professional British soldiers pressed forward.

In the heat of this discouraging summer, a man named Gouverneur Morris (1752–1816) visited the soldiers. Morris was a powerful political leader who later helped

Gouverneur Morris first considered the idea of a canal in the late 1700s.

write the U.S. Constitution. But Morris did not discuss military matters during his trip to the front. Instead, he told the men that someday a canal would cut through New York State and connect Lake Erie with the Hudson River. Gouverneur Morris saw the United States as a country whose people would spread westward over a newly constructed waterway. In a letter written years later he exclaimed, "As yet, we only crawl along the outer shell of our country. The interior excels the part we inhabit in soil, in climate, in everything. The proudest empire in Europe is but a bubble compared to what America will be, must be . . ."

Gouverneur Morris died before work on the canal of his dreams even began. However, other dreamers soon took up the canal's cause. The need for such a waterway increased as the nation gained vast territories in the west.

The American Revolution officially ended in 1783 with the signing of the Treaty of Paris. The treaty gave the new United States all the land west of the Appalachians to the Mississippi River. Twenty years later, the United States

As a result of the Treaty of Paris in 1783, small settlements sprang up along the banks of the Mississippi River.

★ ★ ★ ★

became even larger. In 1803, President Thomas Jefferson bought land from the French in what became known as the Louisiana Purchase. This land stretched from the Mississippi River to the Rocky Mountains. These newly acquired lands became America's western frontier. The nation's leaders hoped that settlers would soon build farms and villages on this raw land.

One such leader was DeWitt Clinton (1769–1828), a big, rugged-looking man who was born into a wealthy New York State family. Clinton was once the mayor of New York City.

In 1803, the United States bought the Louisiana Territory from France. All or part of thirteen states were later formed from this area.

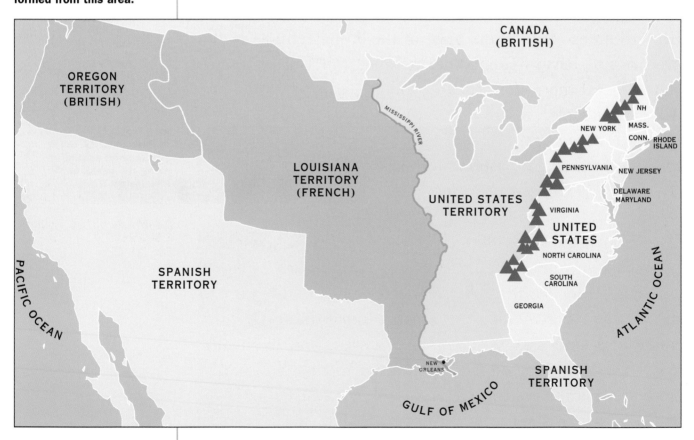

10

As mayor, he did not coop himself up in an office. Instead, he was often seen tugging at hoses with New York's fire crews as they fought the city's frequent blazes.

In the early 1800s, serious talk began about a canal running the width of New York State. At first, DeWitt Clinton joined those who said a waterway through the forests and mountains could not be created. However, Clinton was a **visionary**. He looked to the future and saw rapid population growth for New York State and for the nation. Clearly, the American people, most of whom were farmers, would want to work the splendid land on the western frontier. Over time, Clinton became the canal's most spirited backer. New Yorkers jokingly called the proposed canal Clinton's Ditch.

DeWitt Clinton is sometimes called the "Father of the Erie Canal."

Other New York State residents began to share Clinton's enthusiasm for a canal. A westward canal would have to stretch more than 300 miles (483 km) across the state. If the canal were successful, stores, businesses, and even new towns would develop along the waterway's route. Gradually, more and more New Yorkers agreed that a canal should be built and that it should run across their state.

Thomas Davies painted this illustration of the Hudson River in the 1700s. The river would provide the canal with an outlet to the Atlantic Ocean.

DRAWING UP A PLAN

In 1816 New York State established a canal **commission**. The commission's job was to create a plan for building a westward waterway. The canal plan had to answer several very important questions:

What route should the canal take? A good route would connect the Hudson River with Lake Erie. Ships could take goods from New York City, located near the Atlantic Ocean, to Albany, New York, on the Hudson River. The goods could then be transferred to smaller canal boats for the trip to Lake Erie. Therefore, the waterway would link the Atlantic Ocean with the Great Lakes. Because it would end in Lake Erie, the waterway came to be called the Erie Canal. Upon completion, the Erie Canal measured 363 miles (584 km) in length.

Should the canal be one continuous ditch? Lake Erie is about 565 feet (172 meters) higher than the Hudson River. A continuous canal meant that westward bound boats would have to move uphill. From the beginning, it was decided to build a lock canal. Locks are like giant staircases that allow a boat to be lifted up or down a steep **terrain**.

Who should pay for the canal's construction costs? At first, New York politicians hoped the United States government would help put up the money for construction. But most national leaders still considered the project to be a crazy idea. So New York State decided to bear the

This is a map of the canal, from Albany to Buffalo.

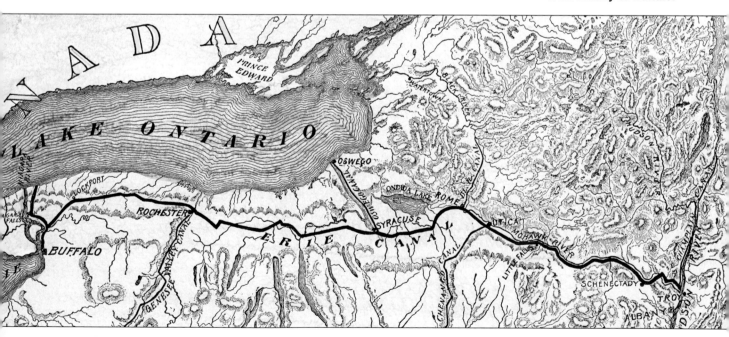

construction costs. After all, every mile of the canal's route was over New York land. Many New York taxpayers were unwilling to finance the venture because of its great expense. Those who wanted to build the canal reminded taxpayers that boats using the waterway were required to pay tolls (fees for passage). It was hoped that toll collection would eventually replace state funds.

DeWitt Clinton was elected governor of New York in 1817. Using all of his political skills, Clinton persuaded the New York State legislature to grant six million dollars to begin construction. At the time, New York State's population was 1.3 million. This meant the initial costs would amount to about five dollars for every man, woman, and child in the state. Most New York workers earned less than five dollars a week, so the canal would cost them dearly.

WORK BEGINS ON CLINTON'S DITCH

On the morning of July 4, 1817, cannons boomed. The cannons, firing near Rome, New York, **heralded** the start of construction on the Erie Canal. It was Independence Day, a proper day to begin a project designed to mold the country's future. The town of Rome was almost in the middle of the canal route. It was decided to start construction there and dig both east and west. Soil samples revealed that the digging would be easy near Rome.

A crowd gathered, and politicians gave speeches. A judge named John Richardson said, "By this great highway

Surrounded by a crowd, Judge John Richardson dug the first shovelful of earth in the Erie Canal project.

unborn millions will easily transport their surplus productions to the shores of the Atlantic . . ." At the end of the speech, Judge Richardson drove his spade into the ground. He **extracted** the first shovelful of earth in what would be the biggest construction project to date in U.S. history.

Though work had started, a thousand details were still unresolved. Few American engineers knew how to build the locks needed to lift canal boats up and down hills and mountains. Such matters would simply have to be dealt with as the digging progressed. Crews were breaking new

★ ★ ★ ★

ground. Never before—not even in their most fantastic dreams—had Americans attempted a construction job as gigantic as this one. American engineers digging the Erie Canal had no choice but to learn "on the go."

The two chief officers in charge of construction were Benjamin Wright and James Geddes. Neither of the men were trained engineers. They were New York lawyers who had experience surveying land. A surveyor measures land to create ownership boundaries. Using their surveying skills, the two lawyers mapped out the course of the ditch. At the start of the project, no one knew exactly where the canal would end. Only after construction began did officials decide to dig the great ditch through to the small town of Buffalo on Lake Erie.

Few people realized how difficult construction would be. Thousands of laborers worked more than ten hours a day to get the job done.

The canal was designed to be 40 feet (12 m) wide at the top and then taper downward to 28 feet (8.5 m) wide at the bottom. The middle of the ditch was to be 4 feet (1.2 m) deep. Canal boats had no sails or power engines. The boats were towed by horses or mules. Therefore, an animal path, called a towpath, was built on one side. Thus the crews

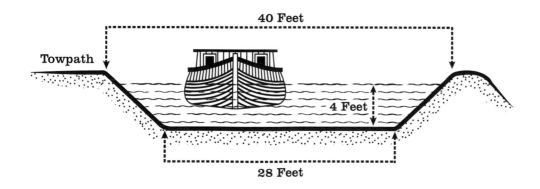

were presented with a challenge: They had to dig a ditch and create a towpath through 363 miles (584 km) of mountains and forests.

In central New York, trees were chopped down and an army of diggers attacked the soil. Most work was done by hand because there were few machines available to assist the laborers. However, machines did make an appearance. Several were good examples of what is often called Yankee ingenuity. This term described the "Yanks" who lived in the eastern states and had an almost magical ability to make something out of nothing.

Simply chopping down a tree left its roots in the ground. Workers then had to do the tiring job of digging through the tangle of roots. One canal worker built a

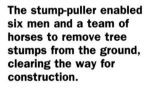

The stump-puller enabled six men and a team of horses to remove tree stumps from the ground, clearing the way for construction.

machine that pulled tree stumps from the earth. The device looked like a giant spool. Crews pushed the spool over a stump. With the help of ropes, chains, and a team of horses, the spool-shaped machine lifted the stump out of the ground, roots and all.

By learning on the go, canal workers overcame other problems. For example, groundwater often seeped into the diggings. A crew would dig a long section during the day, leave the site to sleep, then return in the morning to discover their freshly dug ditch filled with water. In time, the workers learned to line the sides of their ditch with red clay to prevent seepage.

An even better solution to this problem was developed by an assistant engineer named Canvass White. He discovered how to make a special kind of **hydraulic** cement using limestone found in upstate New York. White's hydraulic cement hardened even if it was underwater. Using hydraulic cement, workers were able to protect the canal walls from underground water and even from pouring rain.

WORKERS FROM NEAR AND FAR

At first, work crews were made up mostly of people from upstate New York. Clinton and canal officials reasoned they could win the hearts of New Yorkers by giving them the first crack at jobs. But farmers in rural New York had to return to their fields in the spring for planting and in the fall for harvesting. Work on the canal stopped and

Local workers came and went from the canal depending on the farming season.

started according to needs on the farms. One observer said the canal looked like "a dotted line of poorly dug, unfinished ditches."

The project needed a full-time workforce. However, it was difficult to persuade American workers to leave their families and toil in the wilds along the canal route. So officials looked overseas for workers.

Many laborers came from Ireland. Most people there were poor. Small farmers did not own their own land. Instead, they paid rent to a landlord. Rent payments kept families poor for generations. It is no wonder the Irish began to look to America, where wages were high and land was cheap. One Irish newspaper called the young United States, "the best poor man's country [in the world]."

Penny by penny, Irish families scraped together enough money to pay ship passage for the father or eldest son. The man was then expected to earn enough money in America to pay for the rest of the family to cross the ocean. Most Irish workers were young, strong, and eager to work.

Canal officials went to New York City to meet immigrants coming off the ships. Canal bosses offered laborers eighty

Immigrants arrive at a U.S. port ready to work.

cents a day. Eighty cents for a day's work was considered good wages by U.S. standards. To the Irish, however, the pay was unbelievable. In fact, many Irish immigrants thought they had misheard the officials. They reported to the job thinking they would earn eighty cents a week. By the early 1820s, the canal workforce totaled some nine thousand men. It is believed that at least one-quarter were Irish immigrants.

Work on the canal was grueling. Men worked fourteen-hour days. The summer was stifling. Worst were the swarms of mosquitoes that tormented the diggers. A dismal area in the middle of the canal route called Montezuma's Swamp was a breeding ground for mosquitoes. Local Seneca Indians told crews not to enter the swamp, because of the terrible mosquitoes. The men entered the swamp anyway. According to one report, "[mosquitoes] fell upon the diggers in hordes. The men

German and Irish immigrants joined local farmers and laborers to make up the Erie Canal workforce.

To build a lock, workers used pulley cranes to dig out earth.

came in with eyes swollen almost shut and hands so poisoned that they could hardly wield their tools."

Canal work was also dangerous. Dynamite had not been invented, so crews used gunpowder to blast open rock. This was a tricky process. One mistake caused the gunpowder to blow up on the workers. Work-related accidents took many lives. A newspaper called the *Lockport Observatory* reported the death of one man, Orrin Harrison, who was helping to build a lock. According to the report, he "was leaning against one of the balance beams, and from excessive fatigue fell asleep, and [drowned] in about 8 feet (2.4 m) of water."

Despite the exhausting workload, the men managed to sing as they performed their duties. Their work songs later became the **folklore** of America:

> *We are cutting a ditch through the gravel,*
> *Through the gravel across the state!*
> *We are cutting the ditch through the gravel,*
> *So the people and freight they can travel,*
> *Can travel across the state!*

23

This photograph shows the Schoharie Aqueduct in Fort Hunter, New York.

AQUEDUCTS AND LOCKS

In many places the Erie Canal had to cross rivers. Therefore the crews built bridges, called aqueducts, to carry canal water above rivers and streams. Normally aqueducts transport water intended for drinking or for irrigating crops. Aqueducts on the Erie Canal, however, were designed to carry boats. Water flowing through them could be thought of as paving material on a highway.

A total of eighteen aqueducts were built for the Erie Canal. They looked somewhat like the rain gutters that line

The aqueduct at Rochester was so impressive that artists were inspired to capture its beauty in paintings.

a house roof. Canal crews built their aqueducts in stone. Some of the aqueducts were designed in a classical Roman style and stood on a series of graceful arches. A farmer watching canal laborers erect one aqueduct said the men were "building castles in the air."

Locks presented the canal builders with their most difficult challenge. A lock is a water-filled chamber with a swinging door on either end. When a boat enters a lock, both swinging doors are closed. Above the lock is another chamber filled with water. A valve is opened, and

THE CRESCENT AQUEDUCT

The canal's longest aqueduct was built at the town of Crescent, near Albany. It measured 1,188 feet (362 m) in length.

25

water from the upper chamber is allowed to flow into the lower one. The boat then floats upward until it reaches the level of the upper chamber. In this way a boat is raised lock by lock, until it "steps up" a hill. Boats are lowered down a hill in the same way, with the process reversed.

The greatest lock system was created at a mountain near Buffalo. There the crews built five double locks, which stood one on top of the other like giant steps. The locks lifted boats 66 feet (20 m) over the face of the mountain. The

The Erie Canal required a total of eighty-three locks. This is Lock #17 in Little Falls.

The Lockport locks represent an engineering wonder. Today, they have been preserved as a historic treasure.

town that grew up along that set of locks was called Lockport. A writer visiting Lockport stared in amazement as water literally took boats uphill. "Here [at Lockport] the great Erie Canal has defied nature and used it like a toy."

A total of eighty-three locks were built over the length of the Erie Canal. The locks worked almost perfectly. Even the

★ ★ ★ ★

laborers were awestruck by these watery stepping-stones. They saluted their creation in song:

We are cutting the ditch through the rocks,
Through the rocks across the state!
We are cutting the ditch through the rocks,
And we're finishing her off with locks,
From the rocks across the state!
From the rocks across the state.

PROGRESS AND FRUSTRATIONS

In October 1819, after two years of work, the first section of the Erie Canal was opened for business. It connected the towns of Rome and Utica and stretched a mere 15 miles (24 km) in length. Canal work was going far more slowly than had been predicted. Costs of the project were mounting. Clinton hoped a partial opening would boost the spirits of New Yorkers.

The small, completed section of the canal was exciting to those who watched the opening ceremonies. Kids swam in Erie waters. Families found the canal a delightful place to fish. But critics asked a pressing question: After two years of toil, only 15 miles (24 km) of the canal

Photographed around 1900, these ice-skaters take advantage of the frozen canal.

were completed. How long would it take before all 363 miles (584 km) were ready for use?

In fact, the construction job was making steady progress. Crews busied themselves with thousands of chores. The canal route cut over farm property, dividing many fields. To keep the farmers happy, more than three hundred small bridges were built so that farmwork could continue at a regular pace. A system of gates was also constructed to supply the canal with water. It acted as an emergency drain system during periods of heavy rain. Also, branch canals were dug off the main route to give local farmers access to the canal.

Still, many New Yorkers continued to grumble about the project. Some called the canal Clinton's Folly. In 1822, politicians who were against the canal had grown so strong

The first barges from Buffalo arrive in New York City via the newly-opened Erie Canal.

they defeated DeWitt Clinton's efforts to be renominated as governor. Two years later, Clinton's enemies struck again. They stripped him of his office as a canal commissioner.

Ultimately, Clinton triumphed. By the end of 1824, a large middle section of the canal was operating. Tolls paid by boat owners raised three hundred thousand dollars. Those who had said the canal would never earn a dime were now shamed. In November 1824, DeWitt Clinton was re-elected governor of New York. He would soon **preside** over a ceremony that opened the entire length of the Erie Canal. It was, possibly, the proudest moment of Clinton's life.

THE WEDDING OF THE WATERS

The Erie Canal was officially opened on October 26, 1825, in a ceremony called the Wedding of the Waters. In Buffalo, New York, bands played and Clinton and other politicians gave speeches. Later the officials boarded a canal boat called the *Seneca Chief* and made the first trip from Buffalo to New York City. The boat was drawn along the towpath by four handsome horses. Clinton's craft and four others that

Across New York, crowds gathered to celebrate the opening of the canal in October 1825.

31

★   ★   ★   ★

This lithograph by Archibald Robertson shows the grand celebration of Erie Canal in New York Harbor. The ships are shown with flags flying, smoke stacks billowing, and guns firing to mark the occasion.

CANNON TELEGRAPH SYSTEM

To announce the opening, cannons were lined up along the length of the canal and down to New York City. When Clinton's boat left Buffalo, the first cannon was fired. When the next crew on line heard the report, they fired their gun. In this manner a chain reaction began. Eighty-one minutes later the last cannon was fired in New York City. Then the process began in reverse so that the people in Buffalo would know the cannon telegraph message was received.

followed carried items from Buffalo. One boat held a bear, a beaver, two young deer, and two Seneca Indian boys dressed in traditional costume. All these were symbols of the West meeting the East. The most important **symbolic** items in the boats were two kegs of water from Lake Erie.

At each town along the canal route, the officials stopped to address the crowds and drink toasts. A grand celebration took place on November 4 in New York City. There Governor Clinton poured the two kegs of Lake Erie water into New York Bay, from where it would eventually flow into the Atlantic Ocean. Thus, the bride had been kissed, and the Wedding of the Waters was complete.

Governor Clinton pours a keg of water into New York Bay.

THE CANAL AT WORK

The Erie Canal was the engineering marvel of its time. The artificial river sent boats soaring above land on its aqueducts and allowed boats to climb hills over its locks. Those who said it could not be built stood in wonder as goods and people flowed smoothly through mountains and wilderness. Within two years the canal served two thousand boats, pulled by nine thousand horses, and crewed by eight thousand men.

Perhaps no city benefited more from the canal than did New York City. When the canal was finished, city dwellers heated their homes with coal from western Pennsylvania that was shipped cheaply through the Appalachians on canal boats. New Yorkers also bought wheat that was grown in Ohio and was now sold in city markets at reduced prices. Before the Erie Canal, it cost western farmers one

The Erie Canal also carried tourists who were curious to see the small villages and beautiful countryside of rural New York.

hundred dollars a ton to ship sacks of flour to New York City. When the canal started operating, that cost sank to ten dollars a ton.

The Erie Canal also became a major highway for westward bound settlers. Thousands of New England farm families used the canal to flee the rocky soil of New Hampshire and Vermont and to plow rich land in Illinois and Indiana. Immigrants from Europe rode canal boats and skipped over the eastern United States to settle in the west.

Canal boats were flat-bottomed and about 80 feet (24 m) long by 15 feet (5 m) wide. Most boats had a tiny pilothouse, where the captain stood. This pilothouse had to be low so

A self-propelled canal boat makes its way down the canal in the early 1900s.

Passengers enjoy a leisurely ride on a packet boat.

the vessel could squeeze under the many bridges along the route. Often the boats were run by entire families. The captain ran the boat while his wife cooked and hung washing on deck. Meanwhile, the children pitched in with various chores.

It took seven to ten days for a canal boat to complete the trip from Buffalo to Albany. The pace was so slow that a bored passenger would often step off the boat and walk along the towpath. Then the passenger simply stepped

* * * *

back on the deck and continued his or her trip. The fastest and fanciest boats were passenger vessels called packets. Packet boats were pulled by the finest horses. However, even the swift packets had to observe a canal speed limit not to exceed 4 miles (6 km) per hour.

Along the route, a distinct canal culture arose. Villages developed with restaurants, stores, and hotels to serve passengers and boat crews. A canal language was spoken, too. "Low bridge, everyone down!" meant passengers had to duck because the boat was passing under a bridge with just a foot or two of

WINTER SHUTDOWN

The Erie Canal closed about five months each year as winter temperatures turned the water into ice. For local people the canal became a delightful place to ice-skate. A favorite spot was on the aqueduct at Rochester, where skaters could speed along the surface while looking down on the city's Genesee River.

The towns that grew up alongside the canal had a culture all their own, including language, folklore, and music.

Steam-towing canal boats were introduced in the late 1800s.

clearance. The canal culture inspired many songs, including a lively number belted out by teamsters as they drove animals along the towpath:

*I've got an old mule and her
  name is Sal,
Fifteen miles on the Erie Canal.
She's a good old worker and a
  good old pal,
Fifteen miles on the Erie Canal.
We've hauled some barges in
  our day,
Filled with lumber, coal, and hay,
And every inch of the way
  we know
From Albany to Buffalo.*

The Erie Canal was a financial success for New York State. Within nine years, tolls collected from canal boats repaid the state's construction money. The canal continued to make a profit even into the 1850s and 1860s, when railroads began operating along its route. Cargo such as coal could be shipped cheaper on canal barges than on trains. In 1882 canal tolls were abolished. By that time, the canal had paid for itself many times over.

THE ERIE CANAL TODAY

Almost two hundred years after it opened, the Erie Canal continues to serve New York. It is now part of the New York

State Canal System, which connects many of New York's large natural waterways and lakes. The canal is still a shipping route for goods between the Hudson River and the Great Lakes. It is also a tourist attraction. Canal banks are lined with **marinas** that tend to the houseboats and sport-fishing boats that sail its waters. Scenic bicycle and hiking trails also run along its route. As a result, Clinton's Ditch generates jobs today in the tourist business. Thousands of New York residents work in the restaurants and hotels that cater to boat owners.

The present-day canal looks nothing like it did when it opened long ago. The great ditch was enlarged three times—in 1862, 1895, and in 1918. The enlargements were necessary to allow for passage of bigger boats. The canal is now 120 to 200 feet (37 to 61 m) wide and about 14 feet

Two mules pull a boat filled with tourists at Erie Canal Village, a living history museum about the canal.

Today, many communities around the canal, such as Fairport, shown here, have become tourist attractions.

(4.3 m) deep. These dimensions make the waterway about three times as wide and three times as deep as the original.

Today, history buffs serve as canal detectives. Reconstruction has all but replaced the original canal. Still, the history detectives know those few spots along the route where one can still see patches of brickwork created by the long-ago workers who built Clinton's Ditch. Those **remnants** of the old canal remind us of the poetry, the lore, and the music inspired by this watery highway that opened the American West.

Glossary

commission—a group of people that is put in charge of gathering information about a particular subject

dismal—depressing, sad

extracted—pulled out

folklore—tales and traditional beliefs of a nation or people

heralded—announced with great fanfare

hydraulic—used to describe a substance that hardens underwater

marinas—places such as restaurants or repair stations that provide service to boats and boat crews

preside—to direct or watch over

remnants—pieces left from an older object that serve as
a reminder of that object

symbolic—an object that represents an idea, a belief, or
another object

terrain—an area of land

trekking—making a slow, difficult journey, often by foot

visionary—person who is capable of looking into or
planning for the future

Timeline: The Erie Canal

1783	1803	1809	1811	1816	1817	1819
The Treaty of Paris officially ends the American Revolution. The new United States now owns the land west of the Appalachian mountains to the Mississippi River.	In a transaction called the Louisiana Purchase, President Thomas Jefferson buys 827,987 square miles (2,144,476 sq km) of land from France for about fifteen million dollars.	 President Jefferson rejects the idea of building a westward canal through New York State.	Work begins on the Cumberland Road, an overland route through the Appalachian Mountains.	New York State appoints a canal commission to study construction proposals.	DeWitt Clinton is elected governor of New York. Work on the Erie Canal begins on July 4.	The first section of the canal (15 miles/ 24 km in length) is opened.

44

1820	1822	1824	1825	1827	1882

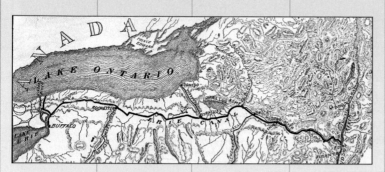

				Some two thousand boats operate on the Erie Canal, giving jobs to about eight thousand crewmen.	Tolls are abolished on the Erie Canal.
About seventy-five canal boats begin operation in the middle section of the canal.	Anticanal politicians defeat DeWitt Clinton's efforts to be renominated as New York's governor.	More than three hundred thousand dollars is collected in tolls paid by canal boats operating on the still unfinished Erie Canal.	In a ceremony called the Wedding of the Waters, the entire length of the Erie Canal is declared officially opened.		

To Find Out More

BOOKS

Bial, Raymond. *The Canals*. Tarrytown, NY: Benchmark Books, 2001.

Harness, Cheryl. *The Amazing Impossible Erie Canal*. New York: Simon and Schuster, 1995.

Lourie, Peter. *Erie Canal: Canoeing America's Great Waterway*. Honesdale, Penn.: Boyds Mills Press, 1997.

Oxlade, Chris. *Canals*. Chicago: Heinemann Library, 2000.

WEBSITES

The Erie Canal Online
www.syracuse.com/features/eriecanal/

The Erie Canal Museum
www.eriecanalmuseum.org/

Erie Canal Village
www.eriecanalvillage.net/

Index

About the Author

R. Conrad Stein was born and grew up in Chicago. At age eighteen he enlisted in the U.S. Marine Corps and served three years. He later attended the University of Illinois, where he earned a degree in history. Mr. Stein is a full-time writer of books for young readers. Over the years he has published more than one hundred books on history and geography subjects.

The author is especially interested in the Erie Canal. He once drove the length of the canal from Albany to Buffalo. During the trip he was awed by the beauty of upstate New York. The author lives in Chicago with his wife, Deborah Kent (also a writer of books for young readers), and their daughter, Janna.